MAINE

by Jonatha A. Brown

GARETH**STEVENS**

A Member of the WRC Media Family of Companies

Please visit our web site at: www.garethstevens.com
For a free color catalog describing Gareth Stevens Publishing's
list of high-quality books, call 1-800-542-2595 (USA) or
1-800-387-3178 (Canada).

Library of Congress Cataloging-in-Publication Data

Brown, Jonatha A.
      Maine / Jonatha A. Brown.
         p. cm. — (Portraits of the states)
      Includes bibliographical references and index.
      ISBN-10: 0-8368-4701-6 — ISBN-13: 978-0-8368-4701-7 (lib. bdg.)
      ISBN-10: 0-8368-4718-0 — ISBN-13: 978-0-8368-4718-5 (softcover)
      1. Maine—Juvenile literature. I. Title. II. Series.
      F19.3.B76   2007
      974.1—dc22   2005036636

This edition first published in 2007 by
Gareth Stevens Publishing
A Weekly Reader® Company
1 Reader's Digest Road
Pleasantville, NY 10570-7000 USA

This edition copyright © 2007 by Gareth Stevens, Inc.

Editorial direction: Mark J. Sachner
Project manager: Jonatha A. Brown
Editor: Catherine Gardner
Art direction and design: Tammy West
Picture research: Diane Laska-Swanke
Indexer: Walter Kronenberg
Production: Jessica Morris and Robert Kraus

Picture credits: Cover, © Pat & Chuck Blackley; pp. 4, 24, 25, 29
© Jeff Greenberg/PhotoEdit; p. 5 © Phil Schermeister/CORBIS; pp. 6, 12
© Bettmann/CORBIS; pp. 7, 9 © North Wind Picture Archives; p. 11 © AP
Images; p. 15 © Gibson Stock Photography; p. 16 © Tom Stewart/CORBIS;
pp. 18, 26, 27 © John Elk III; p. 21 © Paul Rezendes/www.paulrezendes.com;
p. 22 © Spencer Grant/PhotoEdit; p. 28 © James P. Rowan

Printed in the United States of America

2 3 4 5 6 7 8 9 11 10 09 08 07

CONTENTS

Words that are defined in the Glossary appear
in **bold** the first time they are used in the text.

On the Cover: The lighthouse at Pemaquid Point was built in 1835.
Today, its light still warns ships to steer clear of the rocks.

Introduction

What would you like to do in Maine? Eat a big lobster dinner with salt potatoes, corn on the cob, and plenty of melted butter? Visit an old fort that still stands guard over the Penobscot River? Go hiking, canoeing, or whale watching? These are just a few of the things you can do in Maine.

This state is filled with natural beauty. It has ocean beaches, crystal clear lakes, and tree-covered mountains. Many towns have beautiful old homes and charming shops. Museums around the state tell tales of Native Americans, seafaring men, and the people who made this state what it is today. So, come to Maine. You may never want to go home again!

Tourists enjoy the summer sun, sand, and waves at York Beach.

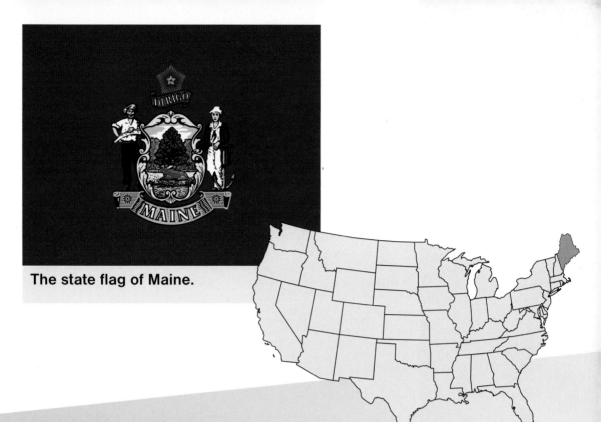

The state flag of Maine.

MAINE FACTS

- Became the 23rd U.S. State: March 15, 1820
- Population (2005): 1,321,505
- Capital: Augusta
- Biggest Cities: Portland, Lewiston, Bangor, South Portland
- Size: 30,862 square miles (79,933 square kilometers)
- Nickname: The Pine Tree State
- State Tree: White pine
- State Flower: White pine cone and tassel
- State Animal: Moose
- State Bird: Chickadee

History

People have lived in Maine for at least ten thousand years. By the 1500s, many small groups of Native Americans lived here. Most of them lived along the Atlantic coast or in river valleys. They hunted deer and caught fish. Some raised crops such as corn, beans, and squash.

John Cabot was probably the first European to reach Maine. He sailed for Britain. Cabot may have reached the coast of Maine in 1498. Twenty-six years later, the French arrived. They were led by Giovanni da Verrazano. He claimed this area for France.

The Penobscot Indians lived in Maine long before the first white explorers arrived. This photo of a Penobscot chief and his family was taken in 1930.

The British wanted land here, too. They began settling in the area in 1607. Their first colony was called Popham Plantation. It was near the Kennebec River. The colony did not last long. After just one year, the British gave up and sailed back home.

Sir Ferdinando Gorges set up Maine's first government in 1636. At about this time, more Europeans arrived, and small villages began to grow along the coast. The winters were harsh, and the soil was rocky. Even so, the settlers stayed. They fished, farmed, and trapped animals for their furs. They cut down trees for lumber. Before long, the whole region became part of a larger colony in the south. This was the Massachusetts Bay Colony.

Fighting for Land and Freedom

Both France and Britain wanted to control Maine. They also wanted the rest of the Atlantic coast. The two countries fought over land for many years. In 1754, the French and Indian War began. The British fought

In the mid-1700s, white men began to explore parts of Maine that lay far from the coast.

IN MAINE'S HISTORY

What Happened to the Natives?

Many thousands of Natives lived in Maine when the first Europeans came to the area. Within just a few years, however, most of the Natives were gone. White people brought diseases with them. Thousands of Natives became ill and died. Others were killed in wars between tribes. Only a few thousand Natives were left in this area by 1620.

the French for nine years. During this war, most of the Natives in Maine fought on the side of the French. Even so, Britain won. Now Britain held thirteen colonies along the Atlantic coast.

The French and Indian War had been very costly. To pay for it, the British king made the colonists pay taxes. Many colonists thought this was unfair. They decided to fight Britain to gain their freedom. The Revolutionary War began in 1775. About six thousand men from Maine fought for freedom. They helped the colonists win the war and form the United States.

Becoming a U.S. State

After the Revolutionary War, Massachusetts wanted to thank its soldiers. It sold land in Maine to them for less than one dollar for each acre. Many settlers moved to Maine to get some of this cheap land.

The United States and Britain fought again in the War of 1812. During this war, the British attacked the coast of Maine. They caused lots of damage there. The people who lived in Maine thought that Massachusetts did not do a good job of protecting them.

In 1819, the people of Maine voted to break away from Massachusetts. They wanted to form a state of their own. The leaders of Massachusetts agreed. The next year, Maine became a U.S. state.

The new state grew. Bath became the biggest shipbuilding center in the nation. Cloth and leather factories were built. Paper, lumber, dried fish, and ice were important products,

FUN FACTS

A First for Maine

In June 1775, a British ship was lurking off the coast of Maine. It was not far from Machias. The ship was the *Margaretta*. Colonists attacked and captured the ship. This was the first sea battle of the Revolutionary War. It was a big victory for the colonists.

By the mid-1800s, more than one thousand sawmills had been built in Maine.

IN MAINE'S HISTORY

Keeping the Balance

In the early 1800s, most Northern states did not allow slavery. The states in the South did. Missouri wanted to join the **Union** as a slave state. The Northern states did not like this idea. They did not want to change the balance between slave and free states. They said Missouri could enter the Union as a slave state only if Maine could enter as a free state. The other states agreed. So, Maine and Missouri became states at the same time. This was the Missouri **Compromise**.

FUN FACTS

Making a Border

For many years, the United States and Britain could not agree on the border between the U.S. and Canada. In 1839, both nations sent soldiers to the Aroostook area of Maine. They were ready to fight a war. The two sides agreed to have one last meeting. Three years later, they signed a treaty that set the border. No shots were fired. Still, this tense time is known as the Aroostook War of 1839.

too. Potatoes became a big crop for the people of Maine.

The Civil War

In 1860, Southern states began breaking away from the Union. They formed their own country. The Northern states did not want to have two nations, so the two sides began to fight. The Civil War lasted from 1861 until 1865. The people of Maine fought on the side of the Northern states. Factories in Maine made supplies for the U.S. Army. The war was awful in many ways, but it helped factories grow.

The North won the war, and Maine kept growing. Railroads were built, and paper and cloth mills grew. In Bath, shipyards began making steel ships.

The 1900s and Beyond

In the first half of the 1900s, the United States fought in two world wars. Maine shipyards made ships and submarines. Factories in the state made boots and uniforms for the soldiers.

In the second half of the century, the U.S. Air Force built bases in the state. **High-tech** companies moved to this area, too. Meanwhile, more and more people came to Maine on vacation. They came to see the

IN MAINE'S HISTORY

Righting a Wrong

Long ago, colonists stole land in Maine from the Native Americans. They did not pay for it. In 1980, the U.S. government agreed that this had been wrong. The government paid the Natives for the land they had lost. The Natives used this money to buy forests and blueberry fields. Now, the Natives of Maine make money from the **timber** and blueberries on their land.

The Bath Iron Works was founded in 1826. It made Bath the nation's leading city for shipbuilding. The Bath Iron Works is still building ships for the U.S. Navy today.

Famous People of Maine

Margaret Chase Smith

Born: December 14, 1897, Skowhegan, Maine

Died: May 29, 1995, Skowhegan, Maine

Margaret Chase Smith was the first woman to serve in both houses of Congress. She served in the U.S. House of Representatives in the 1940s. Then, she was elected to the U.S. Senate. She served there for many years. She was so popular that she ran for U.S. president in 1964. Her party, the Republicans, did not choose her to be their candidate that year. Even so, she was the first woman to seek the presidential nomination of a major political party.

state's lovely coastline and forests. The **tourists** stayed at hotels and inns and ate at restaurants. Thanks to the tourists, these kinds of businesses grew.

Some businesses in the state did not do as well. Fishermen had trouble making a living. Some paper and cloth factories closed, too.

Today, the people of Maine take care of their state. They try to protect the land and water. They want to be sure that Maine will always be a beautiful place to live in and to visit.

★ ★ ★ Time Line ★ ★ ★

1498	John Cabot probably reaches the Maine coast.
1524	Giovanni da Verrazano claims the coast of Maine for France.
1607	The British found the colony of Popham Plantation; it lasts for one year.
1636	Sir Ferdinando Gorges sets up the first government in Maine.
1775	The first naval battle of the Revolutionary War is fought near Machias.
1820	Maine becomes the twenty-third U.S. state on March 15.
1842	A treaty sets the border between Maine and Canada.
1861–1865	Maine fights on the side of the North in the Civil War.
1894	The first railroad in the state is built.
1917–1918	Factories in Maine make war supplies during World War I.
1941–1945	Factories in Maine make supplies for use in World War II.
1948	Margaret Chase Smith is elected U.S. senator from Maine. She is the first woman elected to both houses of Congress.
1980	The U.S. government pays several Native tribes millions of dollars for land stolen from them long ago.

People

Maine has fewer people than most other U.S. states. Fewer than 1.4 million people live here. About six out of every ten of these people live in the country. Most of them live in small settlements and on farms. The rest of the people in Maine live in or near cities. Nearly all of the cities are near the coast.

Portland is the biggest city in Maine. About sixty-five thousand people live there. Lewiston, Bangor, and South Portland are other big cities in the state,

Hispanics

This chart shows the different racial backgrounds of people in Maine. In the 2000 U.S. Census, 0.7 percent of the people in Maine called themselves Latino or Hispanic. Most of them or their relatives came from places where Spanish is spoken. Hispanics do not appear on this chart because they may come from any racial background.

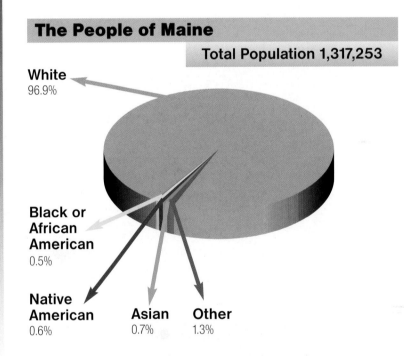

The People of Maine

Total Population 1,317,253

White
96.9%

Black or African American
0.5%

Native American
0.6%

Asian
0.7%

Other
1.3%

Percentages are based on the 2000 Census.

but they are much smaller than the city of Portland.

Yesterday

About twenty thousand Native Americans lived here in 1600. Most of the Natives did not live here long after the whites arrived. Some of them died of disease or in wars. Others moved away.

Most of the early white settlers were from Britain and France. Later, many people moved to this area from Scotland and Ireland.

The city of Portland is located on Casco Bay. Like most of Maine's cities, Portland is in the southern part of the state.

Some settlers came from Canada, too. One of the largest groups from Canada was known as the French Acadians. They moved to Maine after the French and Indian War.

Today

Now, almost 97 percent of the **population** of Maine is white. It includes a large

It is a cool fall day at the University of Maine in Orono. Here, two students are playing chess on the university's leaf-strewn lawn.

group of French Acadians. Some Asians and African Americans live here, too.

About seven thousand Natives still make their homes in Maine. They belong to four tribes. Two of these tribes have **reservations** in the state.

Most people who live in Maine were born in the United States. Few people are now moving here from other countries.

Religion and Education

Most Mainers are Christian. The biggest church in the state is the Roman Catholic church. Many Baptists and Methodists live here, too. Jews and people of other faiths also live in Maine.

In the early days, Maine did not have a system of

public schools. Sometimes, traveling teachers went from town to town. Other times, parents or ministers taught children. The state set up a public school system in 1828. The state's leaders needed to raise money for schools. So they sold timber from lands that were owned by the state. Today, money from that sale still helps pay for schools. But most of the money for education comes from taxes.

Maine has many colleges and universities. The largest of them is the University of Maine. Its main **campus** is in the city of Orono. About twenty thousand students go to school there. The state also has a number of fine private colleges. Two of them are Colby College in Waterville and Bates College in Lewiston.

Famous People of Maine

Hannibal Hamlin

Born: August 27, 1809, Paris Hill, Maine

Died: July 4, 1891, Bangor, Maine

Hannibal Hamlin was a famous lawmaker. He believed slavery was wrong, and he often spoke out against it. The people of Maine elected Hamlin to the U.S. Congress several times. First, he served in the House of Representatives. Then, he served in the Senate. In 1860, Abraham Lincoln ran for U.S. president. He asked Hamlin to be his vice president. The two men were elected, and Hamlin served with Lincoln through most of the Civil War. Hamlin then went back to the Senate. There, he worked for equal rights for African Americans.

The Land

Maine is in a part of the United States known as New England. It is the largest of the six New England states. Maine has warm, pleasant summers. Winters are long and cold. The weather is milder along the coast than it is farther inland.

The Coast

Maine borders on the Atlantic Ocean. Measuring in a straight line, the state's coast is 228 miles (367 km) long. But this coastline is very wiggly. It is filled with bays and coves. Including all of the **inlets**, the state has 3,478 miles (5,597 km) of coast!

★ **FUN FACTS**

A Land Shaped by Ice

Thousands of years ago, huge sheets of ice covered Maine. These ice sheets are called **glaciers**. As the glaciers moved across the land, they sliced tops off mountains and carved beds for rivers and lakes. When the glaciers melted, they left gravel, rocks, and **boulders** behind. They also created more than 5,100 streams and more than 2,200 lakes and ponds.

Most of the Maine shoreline is rocky. This rocky stretch of coast is near Portland.

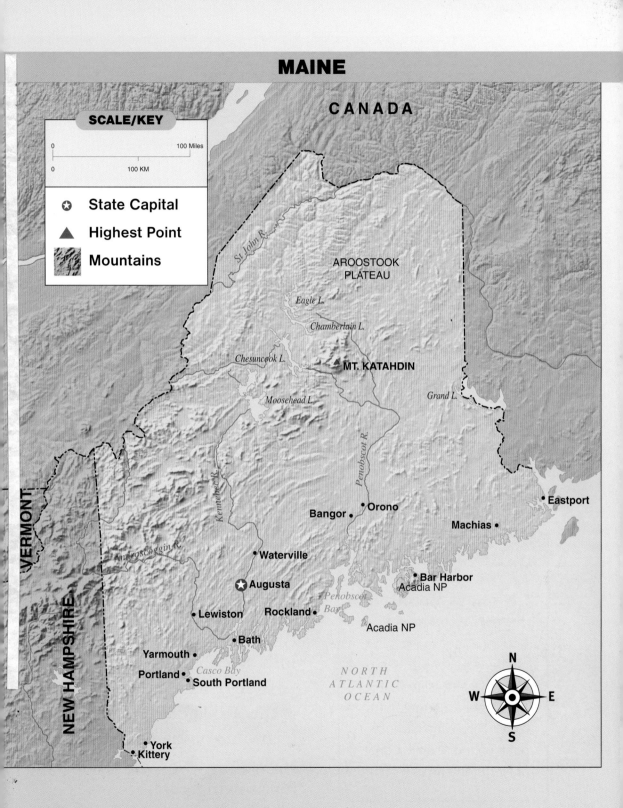

MAINE

SCALE/KEY

0   100 Miles

0   100 KM

⊛ State Capital

▲ Highest Point

▨ Mountains

CANADA

VERMONT

NEW HAMPSHIRE

St. John R.

AROOSTOOK
PLATEAU

Eagle L.

Chamberlain L.

Chesuncook L.

MT. KATAHDIN

Moosehead L.

Grand L.

Kennebec R.

Penobscot R.

• **Eastport**

Bangor • **Orono**

Machias •

Androscoggin R.

• **Waterville**

⊛ **Augusta**

• **Bar Harbor**
Acadia NP

Rockland •
Penobscot Bay

• **Lewiston**

Acadia NP

• **Bath**

Yarmouth •

Casco Bay

Portland •
• **South Portland**

*NORTH
ATLANTIC
OCEAN*

N
W   E
S

• **York**
• **Kittery**

19

Many islands lie just off the coast. Mount Desert Island is the biggest. Part of this island has been set aside as Acadia National Park.

The southern beaches are long and sandy. Farther north, the shore is rockier. In some places, sheer cliffs plunge down to the ocean. The north has fewer sand beaches, and they are not as long as those in the south.

Most of the land along the coast is low and gently rolling. In some places, **salt** **marshes** have formed. Creeks and rivers also cut through the land as they flow to the ocean. Water in these streams rises and falls with the tides, just as it does along the ocean shore.

Major Rivers

St. John River
418 miles (673 km) long

Androscoggin River
157 miles (253 km) long

Kennebec River
150 miles (240 km) long

Upland and Mountains

Inland from the coast lies a region known as the Upland. The land tends to be flat or rolling here. In some places, hills are as high as 2,000 feet (610 m). Part of the Upland is the Aroostook **Plateau**. It has some of the best soil in the state. This soil is good for growing potatoes.

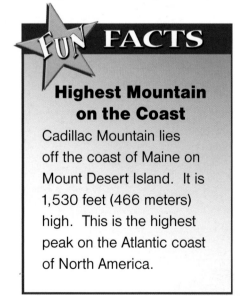

FUN FACTS

Highest Mountain on the Coast

Cadillac Mountain lies off the coast of Maine on Mount Desert Island. It is 1,530 feet (466 meters) high. This is the highest peak on the Atlantic coast of North America.

The White Mountains cover most of western and north-central Maine. Here, the land is much higher than it is in the rest of the state. The state's highest point is Mount Katahdin. Its peak is 5,267 feet (1,605 m) high.

Plants and Animals

About 90 percent of the state is wooded. No other state has this much forested land. One of the most common trees is the state tree, the White pine. Pine trees are so common in the state that Maine's nickname is the Pine Tree State. Spruces, birches, firs, and many other kinds of trees also grow here.

Maine is full of wildlife. It is home to thousands of moose. The moose is the state animal. Bears, deer, bobcats, and many other animals also live in Maine. The state's smaller animals include beavers, raccoons, foxes, and mink.

Maine is famous for its lobsters. These shellfish live in the cold waters of the Atlantic Ocean. Whales live in the ocean near Maine, too. This state is a fine place for whale watching.

A peaceful valley lies at the foot of Mount Katahdin in Baxter State Park.

Economy

Most of the early settlers depended on the land for nearly everything. They cut trees for wood, hunted, fished, and farmed. Today, fewer people in this state work at these kinds of jobs, but they are still important.

More lobsters come from Maine than any other state in the nation. The ocean also provides clams, shrimp, and fish.

Only 3 percent of the land in Maine is farmed. Potatoes and blueberries are the biggest crops. Maine harvests more wild blueberries than any other state. Turkeys, chickens, and dairy cows are also raised here. Eggs and milk are two of the biggest farm products.

Portland has one of the busiest harbors in Maine. Here, tugboats guide a big tanker into the harbor.

Making Goods

Many cities in the state have paper mills. Workers at these mills make paper and cardboard for bags, boxes, and other products. Wood from the state's trees is also made into matches, toothpicks, and other useful items.

Shipbuilding and shipping have long been important here. Bath is still a major shipbuilding center. The biggest ports in the state are Portland, Eastport, and Searsport.

Tourism

Millions of tourists visit Maine each year. They go to museums and parks and spend money at hotels and restaurants. Businesses that help tourists need workers. Tourism provides jobs for many people in this state.

How Money Is Made in Maine

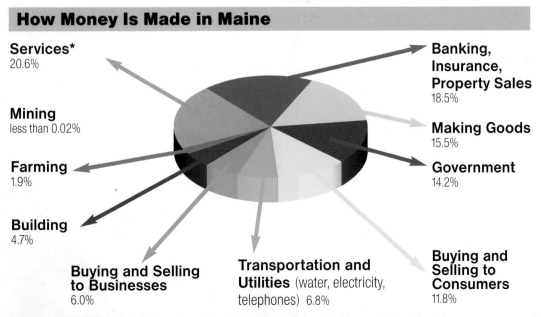

Services* 20.6%

Mining less than 0.02%

Farming 1.9%

Building 4.7%

Buying and Selling to Businesses 6.0%

Transportation and Utilities (water, electricity, telephones) 6.8%

Banking, Insurance, Property Sales 18.5%

Making Goods 15.5%

Government 14.2%

Buying and Selling to Consumers 11.8%

* Services include jobs in hotels, restaurants, auto repair, medicine, teaching, and entertainment.

23

Government

The capital of Maine is Augusta. The state's leaders work there. The state government has three parts. These parts are called the executive, legislative, and judicial branches.

Executive Branch

Many officials work in the executive branch. These officials are led by the governor. This branch makes sure state laws are carried out.

The leaders of the state government meet in the state capitol building.

Blaine House is in Augusta. It has been used as the governor's mansion since 1920.

Legislative Branch

The legislature has two parts. These parts are the Senate and the House of Representatives. These groups work together to make laws for the state.

Judicial Branch

Judges and courts make up the judicial branch. Judges and courts may decide whether people who have been **accused of** committing crimes are guilty.

Local Governments

Maine has sixteen counties. Most counties and towns in the state are run by a team of people. Cities are led by a council and either a mayor or a city manager.

MAINE'S STATE GOVERNMENT

Executive		Legislative		Judicial	
Office	**Length of Term**	**Body**	**Length of Term**	**Court**	**Length of Term**
Governor	4 years	Senate (35 members)	2 years	Supreme (7 justices)	7 years
		House of Representatives (151 members)	2 years	Superior (16 judges)	7 years

Things to See and Do

I f you like adventure and fun, you will love Maine! This state has many wild places. One of them is Baxter State Park. You can pitch a tent in this huge park and go hiking on miles of trails. If you are strong enough, you can even climb Mount Katahdin. It is the highest mountain in Maine.

This state is also home to Acadia National Park. It is one of the most popular national parks in the country. You can go camping, hiking, biking,

Each year, thousands of hikers climb Cadillac Mountain in Acadia National Park. The views from the top are awesome!

swimming, and fishing there. You can climb mountains, too. Most of the peaks offer great views up and down the coast of Maine.

The ocean, lakes, and rivers offer all kinds of water sports. You can rent canoes and kayaks and go fishing. You can also go for a sail and take a boat tour around the coastal islands.

Museums and Historic Sites

The museums in this state offer hours of indoor fun.

You can roam the decks of this old fishing boat at the Maine Maritime Museum in Bath.

Famous People of Maine

Stephen King

Born: September 21, 1947, Portland, Maine

When Stephen King was a child, he liked to write horror stories. His stories told tales of monsters and other scary things. When King grew up, he wrote *Carrie*. It was a very creepy book. People all over the country were frightened and thrilled by it. Before long, *Carrie* was made into a movie. King has written dozens of books since then. Most of them tell horror stories. Stephen King is now one of the most popular writers of our time.

In Augusta, you can visit the Maine State Museum. Some of its exhibits go as far back as twelve thousand years. Others are from colonial days. The Abbe Museum in Bar Harbor focuses on Native Americans who once lived in Maine. It has many displays of **ancient** tools and clothing. The city of Bath has a **maritime** museum. Its exhibits show how shipping helped shape this state over many years.

Fort Knox State Park is near Bucksport. It is a terrific historic site. You can walk through a big old fort that once defended the Penobscot River. In Kittery, you can see beautiful old **mansions**. Other seaside towns also have historic buildings. York even has a historic jailhouse!

If you visit Fort Knox State Park, you will see this huge old gun on display. The fort was built in the mid-1800s.

Famous People of Maine

Samantha Smith

Born: June 29, 1972, Auburn, Maine

Died: August 25, 1985, Auburn, Maine

After World War II, the world had two great powers. One was the United States. The other was the **Soviet Union**. They were enemies. In Auburn, Maine, Samantha Smith worried that the two nations would go to war. She wrote a letter to the Soviet president and told him how much she wanted peace. The president invited her to visit him. Samantha's trip to the Soviet Union was big news all over the world. It reminded people that peace is important to us all. Samantha and her father died in a plane crash shortly after her visit.

A beautiful ship sails through Boothbay Harbor during the Windjammer Festival. This two-day festival is held in Boothbay Harbor every year in June.

Many cities and towns in Maine host festivals every summer. The National Folk Festival is held in Bangor in August. People come from far away to enjoy crafts, toe-tapping music, and storytelling. Other festivals feature the foods Maine is known for. The town of Yarmouth holds a clam festival each July. Union has a blueberry festival in August.

GLOSSARY

accused of — blamed for

ancient — very old

boulders — huge rocks

campus — the grounds that a college is built on

compromise — a kind of agreement in which both parties get less than they want

glaciers — huge, thick masses of ice that move slowly across the land

high-tech — having to do with computers and other advanced kinds of machines

inlets — coves, bays, and the mouths of rivers along the ocean shore

mansions — very large houses

maritime — having to do with ships and the sea

plateau — a large area of flat land that is higher than the land around it

population — the number of people who live in a place such as a state

reservations — lands set aside by the government for a special purpose

salt marshes — swampy areas near the ocean that are sometimes covered with salt water

Soviet Union — a country that once included Russia and other parts of Eastern Europe and Asia

timber — trees that are cut down so the wood can be used

tourists — people who travel for fun

Union — the United States of America

Books

Island Alphabet: An ABC of Maine Islands. Kelly Paul Briggs
(Down East Books)

L is for Lobster: A Maine Alphabet. Discover America State by
State (series). Cynthia Furlong Reynolds (Thompson Gale)

Maine. United States (series). Paul Joseph (Abdo &
Daughters)

Maine: Facts and Symbols. States and Their Symbols (series).
Emily McAuliffe (Hilltop)

Surrounded by Sea: Life on a New England Fishing Island.
Gayle Gibbons (Little Brown and Co.)

Web Sites

Enchanted Learning: Maine
www.enchantedlearning.com/usa/states/maine/

Fun Facts
www.visitmaine.net/funfacts.htm

Maine Historical Society
www.mainehistory.org

Secretary of State's Kids' Page
www.state.me.us/sos/kids/

INDEX